4/95

Our Last Land Giants

Elephants

Our Last Land Giants

Elephants

by Dianne M. MacMillan

A Carolrhoda Nature Watch Book

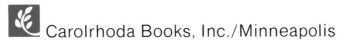
Carolrhoda Books, Inc./Minneapolis

Special thanks to Chuck Doyle, Burnet Park Zoo, for his help with this book.

Metric Conversion

When you know:	multiply by:	to find:
length		
inches	2.5	centimeters
feet	.3	meters
miles	1.60	kilometers
weight		
pounds	.45	kilograms
capacity		
gallons	3.8	liters
temperature		
degrees Fahrenheit	.56 (after subtracting 32)	degrees Celsius

LIBRARY OF CONGRESS CATALOGING-IN-PUBLICATION DATA

MacMillan, Dianne M., 1943-
    Elephants : our last land giants / by Dianne M. MacMillan.
        p.   cm.
    "A Carolrhoda nature watch book."
    Includes index.
    Summary: Text and photos describe the physical characteristics, life cycle, behavior, habitats, and survival problems of the African and Asiatic elephants.
    ISBN 0-87614-770-8 (lib. bdg.)
    1. Elephants—Juvenile literature. [1. Elephants.] I. Title.
QL737.P98M33   1993
599.6'1—dc20   92-35268
                                                                    CIP
                                                                    AC

Manufactured in the United States of America

1 2 3 4 5 6 – P/JR – 98 97 96 95 94 93

To Marianne

In the tall grass on the African plain, a family of elephants feeds noisily. The sounds of chewing and snapping branches break the quiet stillness of the early morning hours. Elephants, the earth's largest land animals, are amazing creatures.

The first of these giant **mammals** and their ancestors, called **proboscideans** (pro-bah-SID-ee-ens), existed more than 45 million years ago and lived all over the world. More than 300 **species,** or kinds, roamed the land. Today, elephants are in danger of becoming **extinct,** or dying out. Thousands of elephants have been killed by humans for their ivory tusks, which are carved to make jewelry and figurines. Also, more people are settling on the lands where elephants live. The animals have less and less land on which they can graze, or feed, making their survival more difficult.

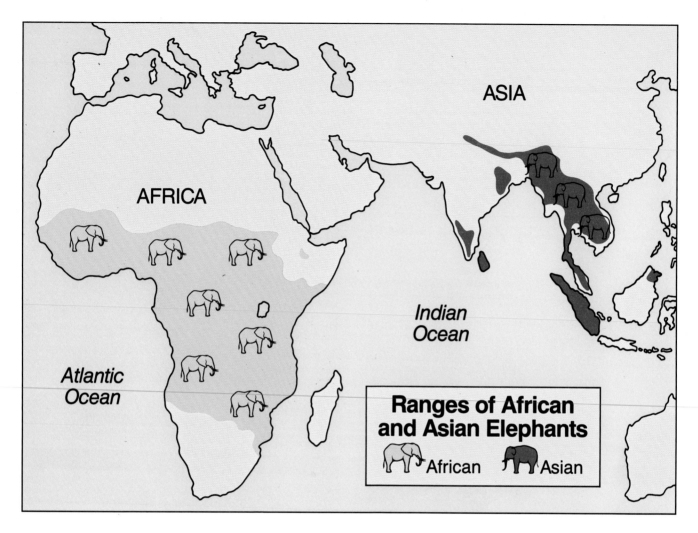

ASIA

AFRICA

Indian
Ocean

Atlantic
Ocean

**Ranges of African
and Asian Elephants**
African   Asian

Today, only two species of elephant exist: African and Asiatic. The scientific name for African elephants is *Loxodonta africana.* The scientific name for Asiatic elephants is *Elephas maximus.*

African elephants, which number less than 600,000, live primarily on **savannas,** or flat, grassy areas, in central and eastern Africa. Much of this land has been set aside as national park **reserves,** which governments have established to protect the wild animals that live there. Asiatic elephants live in the rain forests of India and Southeast Asia. They are more **endangered,** or closer to extinction, than the African species. Only 35,000 to 50,000 Asiatic elephants are left in the wild, some of them on reserves. Another 16,000 live as working elephants. These elephants have been captured and trained to carry heavy loads or perform tricks.

Physical characteristics

African elephants are larger than Asiatic elephants. The males of both species, called **bulls,** are larger than the females, or **cows.** African bulls stand 10 to 12 feet high and weigh about as much as a school bus—from 12,000 to 14,000 pounds. African cows are about 9 feet tall and generally weigh about 10,000 pounds. Asiatic bulls are about as tall as African cows, but they weigh from 7,000 to 11,000 pounds. Asiatic cows are the smallest. They stand about 7 feet high and weigh from 6,000 to 10,000 pounds.

Unlike most other animals, an elephant does not stop growing when it becomes an adult. Elephants grow throughout their entire lives. The larger the elephant, the older it is. Both species of elephant can live to be about 60 years old. However, few elephants ever live out their natural life span. Most elephants are killed, legally or illegally, by hunters.

The African bull is the largest type of elephant.

The large ears of the African elephant (left) are nearly the shape of half circles. The ears of the Asiatic elephant (below) are smaller and are shaped more like triangles.

One of the easiest ways to tell the two species apart is by looking at their ears. African elephants have huge, flapping ears—in fact, elephants' ears are larger than any other animals'. Sometimes they extend 4 feet across. The ears are important for keeping elephants cool in the hot places where they live, because elephants do not sweat as people do. Each ear contains thousands of blood vessels. When an elephant flaps its ears, the fanning motion cools the blood flowing through the ears. This cooled blood then flows through the rest of the elephant's body, lowering its temperature as much as 16°F. The ears of Asiatic elephants are smaller, nearly half the size of African elephants', and they are shaped like a triangle. Since Asiatic elephants live in cooler, forested areas, they do not need such large ears for cooling their bodies.

The creases on this elephant's legs are different than those of any other elephant.

Another difference between the two species is the shape of their bodies. African elephants have swaybacks that dip down in the middle. Asiatic elephants have rounded backs and two bumps on their foreheads.

Asiatic elephants tend to be a lighter gray than African elephants. But because elephants' skin is often covered with mud, its true color is hard to determine.

Every elephant, whether African or Asiatic, has different creases, or folds of skin, on the lower part of its legs. Zoologists (scientists who study animals) can tell one elephant from another by its creases, just as people can be identified by their fingerprints. But most zoologists find it easier to use other characteristics such as ears, tusks, and size to distinguish individual elephants.

Unlike other mammals, African and Asiatic elephants do not have a layer of fat under their skin to protect them from cold temperatures. But because much of their skin is so thick—up to 1 inch—and because they live in tropical areas, staying warm is not much of a problem. If temperatures fell below 35°F, they would not be able to keep their bodies warm for long. As thick-skinned animals, all elephants belong to a group of mammals called **pachyderms** (PAK-ih-durms). *Pachys* is a Greek word that means "thick," and *derma,* also a Greek word, means "skin."

In spite of its thickness and leatherlike appearance, an elephant's skin is quite sensitive to insect bites. Flies and ticks are a constant irritation. Elephants use their trunks to squirt dust over their bodies. They also roll in mud to coat their skin and protect it from insects and parasites. After rolling in the mud, they will scratch their bodies up against trees or rocks to dislodge the ticks.

Despite their thick skin, elephants are sensitive to cold temperatures and insect bites.

12

Rolling in the mud helps elephants stay cool.

Elephants' skin is also sensitive to the scorching sun. To help protect their skin, as well as to stay cool, elephants swim, spray themselves with water, or roll in mud along shallow rivers. Baby elephants, or **calves,** enjoy climbing on top of one another to form a heap of muddy, wiggly elephants. Asiatic elephants like to swim underwater with their trunks in the air like snorkels. In spite of their size, they do not sink to the bottom. They can swim for many hours. African elephants also swim, but they prefer wading in rivers to swimming in deep water.

All African bulls and cows have tusks. Some Asiatic bulls have tusks, but no Asiatic cows do. Tusks are actually two long teeth called **incisors.** The incisors, as well as an elephant's other teeth, continue to grow throughout its life.

African elephants' tusks average 8 to 9 feet in length, and a pair can weigh over 250 pounds. The tusks of Asiatic bulls average 5 to 6 feet in length and can weigh 165 pounds. Elephant tusks are the largest teeth in the animal kingdom.

14

Elephants can use their tusks to protect themselves from danger. But because both species of elephant are generally peaceful animals, they use their tusks most often to dig for water. In dry riverbeds, they will dig down 5 to 8 feet. Then they will wait patiently for water to seep into the hole. Elephants also use their tusks to get food by digging up roots or prying open tree trunks to get to the soft wood inside.

Elephants' tusks are never a matched pair. One is always slightly shorter than the other. Just as humans are right- or left-handed, elephants appear to be right- or left-tusked. The shorter tusk has been worn down because it is the one the elephant uses the most.

Tusks come in handy when digging for water.

Besides their tusks, both species of elephant have four other teeth, called **molars.** Jagged ridges form the tops of the molars. Elephants grind their food back and forth across these ridges instead of chewing up and down, as humans do. An elephant spends from 16 to 18 hours chewing the 300 to 500 pounds of the grass, leaves, bark, and other plant food it needs each day. (That's 125 times as much as the average human adult eats!) This amount of food contains twice the nutrition elephants need, but their digestive systems are not very efficient. Half of the food they eat passes through their bodies without being broken down, or **digested,** so they eat twice as much to make sure they get enough nutrition. Elephants also need about 30 gallons of water every day.

Elephants' strong, sharp teeth allow them to feed on tough branches as well as tender dry grasses.

The large molars of this skeleton indicate that the elephant had grown its sixth and last set of teeth before it died.

Chewing all that food is hard on an elephant's teeth. When one set of teeth wears out, another set grows in from the back of the mouth. An elephant grows six sets of teeth during its lifetime. Each set is larger than the last because the elephant's mouth has grown. The last molars are about 1 foot long and may weigh up to 10 pounds each. An elephant gets its last set of teeth after the age of 30. When that set wears out at around age 60, the animal will no longer be able to chew and will starve to death. However, these days few elephants live long enough to wear out all their teeth.

Because of its many uses, the trunk is very important to an elephant's survival. When it charges, an elephant rolls its trunk under its body.

The trunk, or **proboscis** (pro-BAH-sis), is the most recognizable part of any elephant's body. An outgrowth from the animal's nose and upper lip, it looks like a huge snake and can extend about 6 feet and weigh around 300 pounds.

The trunk has no bones or joints but contains more than 100,000 muscles and tendons (tissues that connect the muscles to other body parts). These muscles and tendons make the trunk both flexible enough to pick up a single flower and strong enough to lift a heavy log.

The end of this African elephant's trunk has two knobs that work together much like humans' fingers to pick up small objects.

On the end of its trunk, an African elephant has two knobs that work like fingers. An Asiatic elephant has only one knob. Elephants use these knobs to pick up their food and put it into their mouths. With their trunks raised, elephants can reach 15 to 20 feet up into the trees to pull off leaves and bark, just as if the trunk were a hand. The trunk can also hold as much as 2 gallons of water at one time. Then the elephant squirts this water into its mouth or showers it over its body.

Adult elephants may use their trunks as weapons to protect baby elephants from predators such as lions, tigers, hyenas, and crocodiles. Adult elephants have no natural predators other than humans.

As the animal's nose, the trunk provides elephants with a highly developed sense of smell. The nostrils are in the tip of the trunk. Just like sailors on a submarine who raise a periscope to see above water, elephants raise their trunks over their heads to sniff the air high above. If the wind is blowing in the right direction, they can detect the presence of one person two miles away.

The trunk also gives elephants a highly developed sense of touch. The sensitive trunk can determine whether an object is hot or cold and what the object's shape and texture are. In swamps or areas where there is quicksand, the trunk allows an elephant to feel its way before taking each step. Since an elephant's eyes are located on the sides of its head, it cannot see the ground directly below it.

This elephant is feeling the ground with its trunk as it moves.

In spite of their size, elephants are graceful circus performers. Most circus elephants are Asiatic, but a few are African.

Elephants' legs are large and strong in order to support the weight of their large bodies. In spite of their size, both species of elephant can move at amazing speeds. For short distances, they can run at 25 miles per hour—almost twice as fast as people can run. More often, they move at about 6 miles per hour. Elephants cannot trot or gallop, because they move both legs on the same side at the same time. The back foot steps on the exact spot where the front foot just stood. Elephants also cannot jump. But if you've ever seen circus elephants perform, you know that elephants have excellent balance. They can walk on their toes and hardly make a sound. A large pad under the toes helps carry their weight.

Communication

African and Asiatic elephants are **nomadic,** or wandering, creatures that move around together in **family units** of 10 to 15 related cows and their calves. All family members follow the lead of the oldest cow, called the **matriarch.** She makes the decisions about where to find food and when to stop and rest.

Elephants communicate these decisions, as well as other messages, through sound, movement, and touch. Experts believe they may make as many as 20 different sounds. The most familiar is a loud, shrill sound called **trumpeting.** They also rumble, grunt, scream, and purr.

When a family unit is moving, members usually follow the matriarch. She is easy to pick out because she is the oldest, and therefore largest, cow.

These elephants show they are angry by holding their ears out from their bodies and trumpeting as they charge. Adult elephants have no reason to be afraid of anything but humans, since they have no natural predators, or animals that hunt them. (Some people believe that elephants are afraid of mice, but it's not true.)

Scientists have recently discovered that elephants also make sounds that are below the range humans can hear. Scientists call these sounds **infrasonic.** These low-pitched sounds may travel up to 3 miles and last for 10 to 15 seconds. Elephants use them for special purposes, such as for mating or for alerting their family unit or a nearby **herd** of danger. Many times, a family of grazing elephants suddenly comes to attention and stands silently still. After a few seconds, the group begins to run very fast in a tight formation, barely making a sound. Very likely, an infrasonic call from an elephant far away has alerted them to some danger. Infrasonic calls also explain why scientists have observed family units from many different parts of a reserve arriving at the same place at the same time.

Elephants also use their ears to communicate. The matriarch will flap her ears and give a soft rumble when she moves or stops to signal her family unit to do the same. Families greet one another with ear flapping and loud rumbles. When an elephant holds its ears out from its body, either it is frightened or it is angry and ready to charge. If its ears are flat against its body, an elephant feels calm and safe. But even then, its ears are seldom still.

Stroking, touching, and rubbing up against one another are other ways elephants communicate. Often, two elephants will stand facing one another with their trunks entwined, or twisted together. When elephants approach one another, they raise their trunks in the air. Then, briefly and gently, each touches the tip of its trunk to the forehead of the other as they pass by. At the same time, they make a rumble that is part of this "greeting ceremony." An elephant may also put the tip of its trunk into another elephant's mouth.

Entwining their trunks seems to be a way elephants show affection for each other.

A bull mates with an estrus cow

Life cycle

Communication is important in elephants' mating process. A cow in **estrus,** the time when she is able to become pregnant, uses infrasonic calls to let bulls in the immediate area know where she is. The oldest and strongest bull mounts the cow and mates with her. He may stay with her for a day or two and mate several more times. After mating, the bull has no further interest in the cow or the calf that will be born, and leaves the family unit. A healthy cow will give birth to a calf every four or five years from the time of first estrus, which usually occurs between ages 10 and 13, until around age 50.

Young bulls reach **puberty**, the time at which they become able to mate, at age 9 to 15, but they do not compete with older bulls for cows. Generally, bulls do not mate until their mid-twenties.

Beginning late in their twenties, bulls begin to go through a condition called **musth** (MUHST). This condition happens once a year and lasts from one week, in younger bulls, to several months, in older bulls. During this time, bulls become more aggressive and release a dark, smelly substance from the sides of their heads. Musth bulls spend their days looking for cows to mate with.

While in musth, a bull will challenge a larger and more dominant bull for the right to mate. Because of this aggressive behavior, smaller bulls that are in musth can sometimes successfully challenge larger bulls not in musth. All bulls are more likely to mate when they are in musth, although they mate at other times as well. They mate with many different cows during their lives.

This bull shows aggressive behavior by the position of his ears and the sounds he makes.

The young elephant in the center remains close to its mother even after the mother has given birth to another calf. The older sibling will help its mother care for the new baby.

Gestation, the time needed for the calf to develop inside its mother before it is born, lasts 22 months. This gestation period is longer than that of any other animal. Elephants are so large that it is difficult to tell if a cow is pregnant. The only outward sign occurs right before birth, when a pregnant cow's two breasts, located between her front legs, swell. Sometimes, milk may begin to drip from the breasts, a sign that the birth is near.

Shortly before giving birth, a pregnant cow appears restless. An older daughter or sister stays close by to help her. The cow remains standing, and at the moment of birth, the newborn baby elephant drops, hind feet first, from its mother's body to the ground below. For a few seconds, the newborn lies still. Then the baby elephant tries to stand. It is pushed by **instinct,** an ability to perform different behaviors without being taught or learning from experience. Somehow, the calf naturally knows that it must stand to reach its mother's breasts for milk. The newborn struggles and falls. Finally, the mother and her helper steady the calf with their trunks so it is able to stand and nurse.

29

These young calves have not yet lost their brown hair.

Newborn calves weigh between 200 and 250 pounds and are about 3 feet tall. Their skin is covered with soft, brown hair, much of which will fall off in a few months. The backs of their ears are pink. They have small tusks called **milk tusks** that are no more than 2 inches long. At around six months to one year old, calves' milk tusks fall out, and they begin to grow their permanent ivory tusks.

About an hour after the birth, the family unit begins to move again, and the newborn must learn to walk. The family moves slowly for the first few days until the calf's legs are strong enough to keep up.

A newborn calf is usually small enough to stand underneath its mother, making it easy to nurse and find safety.

A calf spends the first few months of its life in constant contact with its mother—touching, rubbing, suckling, or being touched by the mother's trunk. After a few weeks, it might wander a short distance away from its mother, but it will race back squealing if it is frightened.

Newborn elephants need a great deal of milk. They nurse as often as five times an hour. By six months of age, calves begin to eat plants, but mother's milk is still the main source of nourishment. A calf will continue to nurse for three to four years, until a new baby brother or sister is born. In comparison, human babies nurse for an average of 7 to 10 months. If the mother dies before a calf reaches two years old, chances are likely that the calf will die also. If the calf is older than this when it is orphaned, one of the other cows in the family will look after it.

Newborn elephants have a lot to learn before they are able to take care of themselves. Unlike other animals, they have a long childhood and spend the years from 2 to 12 learning how to be elephants. They depend on adult family members to teach them. An elephant is not considered to be an adult until around the age of 20. This long childhood is unusual in the animal kingdom and is similar only to humans.

One of the skills a calf must learn is how to control its trunk. A young calf swings its trunk from side to side like a floppy hose and trips over its trunk as it walks. Sometimes, a calf sucks on the end of its trunk the same way a human baby sucks its thumb. When a calf is trying to feed itself, the grass is just as likely to end up on the calf's head as in its mouth. To drink water, a calf will kneel down and drink from a river or lake using its mouth. After some practice, a calf will learn the proper way of sucking up water through its trunk and squirting it into its mouth.

Until a calf learns to use its trunk, it uses its mouth to pick up food.

Through daily play, young bulls learn who is stronger.

Calves spend a large part of each day playing and charging one another. Female calves lose interest in charging as they grow older. But male calves continue to enjoy this play. If their fighting becomes serious, the mothers break it up. By the time the male calves leave the family unit, they know who is stronger in the male social order. The weaker bulls always give way to the stronger ones.

Young bulls leave the family unit when they reach puberty. Usually, young bulls leave by their own choice. Sometimes, an older female will chase them away. The bulls stay alone or with other bulls, sometimes within a few miles of a herd.

Asiatic work elephants are trained to stack logs (left). *They develop close relationships to their mahouts* (below).

Asiatic calves that will be trained as work elephants are captured at around age 5, once they are independent of their mothers. The young elephants require another six to ten years of working with their trainers, or **mahouts** (muh-HOWTS), before they are put to work in the lumber industry in Southeast Asia. During these years of training, elephants learn more than 30 different voice commands and practice hauling and stacking logs.

The bond that develops between the trainer and the elephant is strong. In fact, the elephant comes to know its mahout so well that it can recognize its mahout's call. Working elephants are allowed to roam the jungle at night to find their own food. In the morning, the mahouts call their elephants home.

Family behavior

The elephant family unit plays an important role in the survival of its members, providing protection, nurturing, and companionship. Older sisters and aunts help mothers take care of the calves. If the family unit detects danger, it will form a circle around the young ones. Spreading their ears, the adults will face outward from the circle to create a wall of protection for the youngsters.

Elephants show interest in the remains of dead elephants, whether or not the body is that of a relative.

Family members will also surround an elephant that is injured or sick. With their trunks and bodies, they help the sick one to keep standing. Elephants know that if a sick elephant falls down, it may not have the strength to lift its huge body. When it does fall, the animal's weight will press against its lungs, causing it to suffocate. If an elephant is near death, its family will not abandon it. The others stay nearby, stroking the sick elephant and bringing food and water to place in its mouth.

When a family member dies, the other elephants will frequently cover the body with tree branches and earth. The closest family members usually stay near the body for a day or so. If a herd comes across elephant bones, it will stop to sniff and stroke them. Elephants ignore the bones or remains of other animals.

As cows and their calves wander from place to place, they stay with their family units, searching for food together. They like to feed in the early morning and in the evening, when it is cooler. After waking from their night's rest

36

around 3:00 in the morning, they will feed until daybreak. At daybreak, they move slowly toward a shady area, feeding and drinking along the way. During the hottest part of the day, they rest. The calves lie down on the ground. The adults sleep standing for short periods. They hang their heads down and rest their trunks on the ground or drape them over one of their tusks. As the sun goes down, they begin to move again.

When food is easy to find, family units will gather in herds to socialize.

During the rainy season, grass and other plants are plentiful, so elephants do not need to search constantly for food. Both species of elephant will travel 6 to 9 miles a day. Numerous family units will gather, sometimes creating herds of 500 or more animals. They exchange a great number of greetings, and the calves play together.

In times of drought, finding food and water become the elephants' primary concerns. Individual families seek out their own areas to feed. They may travel up to 30 miles a day searching for food.

During these droughts, few elephants come into estrus or musth, and few calves are born. Calves that are born during drought years have a higher death rate than calves born during periods of normal rainfall. Often the mothers are so weak from lack of food and water that they cannot produce enough milk for their calves. At this point, the matriarch's experience in finding food becomes vital for her family's survival.

Human settlement in the elephant's habitats, like this village in Sri Lanka, makes it harder for elephants to find food and water.

Our last land giants

The future of elephants is uncertain. Both African and Asiatic elephant populations are suffering because too many people live in the areas where they need to roam, and too little food is available.

Elephants need large areas of land to find enough food. As people build more cities, farms, and roads on the African savannas and in Asian rain forests, elephants have less space to find food and water.

In the wild, a natural balance exists between the number of animals and the amount of vegetation, or plant life. By moving from area to area, elephants give the plants they feed on a chance to grow back. But even on reserves, where hunting, farming, and building are not allowed, the amount of land available is not always enough to support the elephants' appetites. When confined to a limited area, they are forced to graze too long in one place, causing permanent damage to the trees and other plants that grow there.

The ticks and insects on elephants' skin provide these birds, called white cattle egrets, with the food they need. In exchange, the egrets warn elephants of danger. Scientists call this relationship, in which two different species help each other survive, symbiosis (sim-bee-OH-sis).

Elephants can cause major damage when they wander into human settlements like this tourist camp in Kenya.

To satisfy their hunger, elephants must sometimes leave the reserves to find food. They often follow the same paths their mothers showed them when the land was unpopulated. In areas where there are now farms or grazing cattle, this causes problems. Sometimes the elephants pass through villages, caving in roofs of houses and buildings in their search for food. In some countries, the government reduces the size of herds by a method called **culling**. Culling is a process of legally killing a certain number of elephants each year. Some people believe killing elephants for any reason is cruel. Others believe culling is necessary to keep elephants from destroying crops and homes and to prevent them from starving to death.

In the last 10 years, the slaughtering of elephants by humans has reduced the elephant population in Africa by 50 percent. In 1989, officials estimated that **poachers** illegally killed 200 African elephants every day for their tusks. Poaching destroys the elephant family unit. Because older elephants have larger tusks, poachers kill them first. This means most of the cows and bulls killed are in their prime mating years. And because of their long gestation period, cows cannot reproduce fast enough to make up for those killed. Young elephants are left without older relatives to teach them elephant ways. They do not have enough experience to survive the cycle of droughts, and they, too, may die early deaths. Some Asiatic elephants are also killed by poachers. But most Asiatic elephants killed illegally are shot by farmers protecting their crops.

Usually poachers kill elephants for their ivory tusks, but other parts of the elephant, like the leg used to make this table, are sometimes used as well.

43

GREAT OBJECTIVES OFTEN REQUIRE
GREAT SACRIFICES. I NOW CALL UPON
THE PEOPLE OF THE WORLD TO JOIN
US IN KENYA BY ELIMINATING THE
TRADE IN IVORY ONCE AND FOR ALL.

H. E. PRESIDENT DANIEL T. ARAP MOI
C.G.H., M.P.

In January 1990, a ban on the international trade of elephant ivory went into effect. It is now illegal to make or sell ivory products. Many people hope the ban will save the remaining wild elephants. African herds in some areas appear to be growing slightly. Still, people need to continue to find ways for humans and elephants to live together. Scientists are sending many more elephants to zoos, where they are trying special programs to help the elephants reproduce. Humans must find ways to help elephants survive so that future generations of people will know the grandeur, intelligence, and magnificence of elephants.

GLOSSARY

bulls: adult male elephants

calves: baby elephants

cows: adult female elephants

culling: the legalized killing of elephants to keep herd sizes down

digested: broken down into simple substances the body can use

endangered: in danger of becoming extinct

estrus: a period of a few days during which female elephants are able to become pregnant

extinct: having no members of a species left alive

family unit: the group made up of 10 to 15 related cows and their calves, which live together

gestation: the period of development before birth

herbivores: animals that eat only plants and no meat

herd: a group created when numerous family units gather

incisors: sharp or pointed front teeth used for cutting

infrasonic: below the range of sound that humans can hear

instinct: a behavior that is inherited rather than learned

mammals: animals with hair or fur that produce milk to feed their young

mahouts: people who train elephants to perform heavy work

matriarch: a female leader

musth: a period of aggressive activity during which bulls fight each other and seek out cows to mate with

nomadic: wandering from place to place

pachyderms: large, thick-skinned, hoofed mammals, such as the elephant, rhinoceros, and hippopotamus

predators: animals that hunt other animals

proboscideans: large, long-snouted mammals belonging to the scientific order Proboscidea

proboscis: a long, flexible snout or trunk

puberty: the stage at which an animal becomes physically able to mate and produce young

reserves: lands that have been reserved, or set aside, for wild animals

savanna: a flat, grassy area in a hot, dry climate

species: a group of plants or animals that have similar characteristics

trumpeting: a loud, shrill sound that elephants make

INDEX

Diagram on p. 8 by Laura Westlund. Photographs courtesy of: front cover, p. 20, Ana Laura Gonzalez; back cover, pp. 16, 19, 28, 35, Bob Zehring; p. 2, Horizons Unlimited Travel Service; pp. 3, 40, Drs. A. A. M. van der Heyden; pp. 5, 34 (right), 44 (right), Minneapolis Public Library; pp. 6-7, 9, 33, 42, Alan Briere; p. 10 (left), S. Dimmitt; pp. 10 (right), 11, 27, 31 (both), 44 (left), Frederic Siskind; pp. 12, 13, 14, 18, 24-25, 26, 38-39, 45, Lex Hes; pp. 15, 34 (left), 36 (left), Frank S. Balthis; pp. 17, 23, 29, 32, 36-37, 41, Gerald & Buff Corsi; p. 21, R. E. Barber; p. 22, Ellie Tyler; p. 30, courtesy of Ringling Bros. and Barnum & Bailey Combined Shows, Inc.; p. 43, Sallie Sprague.

ABOUT THE AUTHOR

"Nature's great masterpiece, an elephant." The words of the poet John Donne rang in her ears as **Dianne MacMillan** read an article from the World Wildlife Fund about elephants. At the time, zoologists predicted that these magnificent animals would be extinct by the year 2000. Although new elephant protection laws have caused this prediction to be lifted, the alarming news compelled Ms. MacMillan to tell children all about these gentle, sociable animals.

A former teacher, Ms. MacMillan has published numerous articles and books for young people. She lives in Anaheim, California, with her husband, Jim, and the youngest of her three daughters.